Harrods
KNIGHTSBRIDGE

WORLD OF
T E A

A Book for Connoisseurs

HAFIZUR RAHMAN
SENIOR TEA BUYER, HARRODS

CONTENTS

FOREWORD 5

INTRODUCTION 6

THE BIRTH OF TEA 10

HARRODS & TEA 14

THE TEA JOURNEY 20

HARRODS INDIAN TEAS 28

HARRODS SRI LANKAN

  (CEYLON) TEAS 46

HARRODS CHINA TEAS 50

HARRODS INFUSIONS 54

THE PERFECT CUP OF TEA ... 58

A GUIDE TO TRADEMARKS ... 62

INDEX 64

HERITAGE

WORLD OF TEA

WORLD OF TEA
A Book for Connoisseurs

FIRST PUBLISHED IN GREAT BRITAIN 2005
BY HARRODS LTD, KNIGHTSBRIDGE, LONDON SW1X 7XL

© HARRODS LIMITED 2005
© PARSONS PUBLISHING 2005

ISBN 1 86464 167 3

PRODUCED AND DESIGNED BY PARSONS PUBLISHING
PRINTED IN HONG KONG BY EVERBEST

THE RIGHT OF HAFIZUR RAHMAN TO BE IDENTIFIED AS THE AUTHOR OF THIS
WORK HAS BEEN ASSERTED IN ACCORDANCE WITH THE COPYRIGHT, DESIGNS
AND PATENTS ACT, 1988.

1 3 5 7 9 8 6 4 2

VISIT HARRODS AT www.harrods.com

FOREWORD

sk anyone who has visited Harrods what it was they enjoyed the most, and I am sure that some would say the Egyptian Escalator; some the Toy Department; others, the Pet Shop; and others still the Ladies Shoe Department! But I guarantee that almost everyone you ask will have been impressed by the Food Halls.

It is no coincidence that the Food Halls are so spectacular — they were built in a lavish style to make a real statement when the new store was constructed some 100 years ago. But why were they built on such a grand scale, I hear you asking?

Harrods is unique for many reasons. It is not the oldest department store in the world, nor the biggest — it is, however, the only department store that started its life by selling food: more specifically, Charles Henry Harrod was a tea merchant. So, when construction of the new store began in 1901, instructions were given to make the Food Halls spectacular in every way to pay homage to the origins of Harrods' success.

We are very fortunate at Harrods to employ many experts in a wide variety of fields — but none more so than Hafizur Rahman, who is our Senior Tea Buyer. Mr Rahman has a wealth of experience from many, many years in the tea industry and has won worldwide acclaim for his knowledge of this very special commodity.

In this book, he shares his expertise with the reader and takes them on a journey that spans some 4,700 years. I hope you will enjoy it.

Mohamed Al Fayed
Chairman

INTRODUCTION

arrods, the world's most famous and exclusive department store, is a name recognised all over the world. With a heritage and tradition second to none, Harrods is a unique institution at the very heart of British society. For over 150 years, it has enjoyed the patronage of the aristocracy, the rich and famous, and has delighted shoppers and sightseers from all over the world.

Its first customer account holders included the writer, Oscar Wilde, and the Shakespearian actress, Ellen Terry. Among the company's other notable points of interest, Harrods installed Britain's first escalator in 1898; it sold A.A. Milne the original Winnie-the-Pooh; and even embalmed Sigmund Freud. Few companies come close to matching the unique status of Harrods. And, from the day the store first opened its doors in 1849, tea has been central to Harrods' culture of retail success.

A heritage and tradition second to none.

Inspired to honour the founder's memory as a fine tea merchant, the Chairman of Harrods, Mr Mohamed Al Fayed continues the store's great tradition by ensuring that in tea, as in everything else, Harrods offers its customers the very best.

With Mr Al Fayed's encouragement, experienced tea buyers from Harrods seek out the world's finest teas, importing exclusive speciality teas directly from selected tea gardens.

The five-strong team of talented and enthusiastic specialists in the Harrods Tea Department are driven by a passion to source superb teas from around the world. They work with the growers to create captivating teas with unique character and quality, appreciated by fine tea connoisseurs worldwide.

In 1999, Harrods was awarded a unique Certificate of Excellence by the Tea Board of India — proof that 150 years after Charles Henry Harrod first sold tea to discerning London shoppers, Harrods is still the best place to experience the perfect brew.

With more than 160 splendid varieties on offer, the range and quality of teas is unparalleled. As a result, more than 2,500 customers a day take the opportunity to select, experiment, and enjoy the world's most perfected teas, from the world's finest tea emporium.

Still the best place to experience the perfect brew.

THE BIRTH OF TEA

Tea is a magical product. The Chinese poet Lu Tíung wrote:

The first cup moistens my lips and throat;
The second cup breaks my loneliness;
The third cup searches my barren entrail
but to find therein some five thousand
volumes of odd ideographs;
The fourth cup raises a slight perspiration —
All the wrongs of life pass out
through my pores:
At the fifth cup I am purified;
The sixth cup calls me to the realms
of the immortals;
The seventh cup — ah, but I could take
no more:
I only feel the breath of the cool wind
that rises in my sleeves.
Where is paradise?
Let me ride on this sweet breeze
and waft away thither.

Legend tells us that 4,700 years ago, the Chinese emperor Shen Nung rested under a camellia tree while some water boiled. A few leaves from the tree fell into the pot. Intrigued, he tasted some of the resulting brew and pronounced it delicious. The drink, *tcha*, was born.

Tea consumption quickly became an integral part of Chinese culture, and was later introduced to Japan by Buddhist priests. By the 1500s, the graceful "tea ceremony" was a highly evolved ritual in imperial Japanese society.

Many people believe that Marco Polo was responsible for tea's arrival in Europe, but the evidence suggests that it was the Portuguese who opened up the first trade routes to China, and introduced tea to Europe in the late sixteenth century.

At this time, Europeans were unsure how to prepare this new herb, and some advice even sug-gested it should be boiled, salted, buttered, and eaten!

The English king, Charles II, who had been exiled to Europe, and his Portuguese wife, Catherine of Braganza, were both tea drinkers. When the monarchy was re-established in England in 1660, tea rapidly became the fashionable afternoon drink.

Although it was an expensive commodity, and was heavily taxed, 240,000 pounds of tea were being imported annually by 1708.

In 1784, the tax on tea was slashed from 119 percent to 12.5

percent to curb tea smuggling. This delicious golden beverage finally became a drink that everyone in Britain could enjoy.

... a drink that everyone could enjoy.

HARRODS & TEA

harles Henry Harrod was born in Essex in 1799. He began trading as a wholesale grocer and tea merchant in 1834 in Stepney, in London's East End.

Through excellent service and careful selection of produce, the business prospered and, in 1849, Harrod acquired a small grocer's shop at 8 Middle Queen's Building (now Brompton Road, Knightsbridge).

HARRODS, Limited, Brompton Road, London, S.W.

TEA DEPARTMENT.

NEW SEASON TEAS,

"The Stores' Mixture."

This is a blend of carefully selected Ceylon, India and China Teas, of really **extraordinary** value, far exceeding in quality any other **Teas** sold at the price.

We offer every facility for testing the value of this splendid Tea, and will be pleased to forward a **Free Sample** if required.

Per lb. ... **1/8** 4 lbs. ... **6/7** 7 lbs. ... **11/8**
Tins (Tins), 20 lbs. nett ... **£1 11s. 8d.**

THE BEST VALUE IN THE KINGDOM.

Tasting Samples Free on Application.

7 lbs. and upwards packed and sent carriage paid to any part of the United Kingdom.

TEA (20 lb.) PACKAGES FREE.

We are now supplying (20 lbs.) packages of Tea in extra thick tins (fine free) in place of wooden caddies; these tins will be found very useful for other purposes when empty.

Carriage Paid to any Part of England, Wales, Scotland, or Ireland.

EXPORT ORDERS.—See Special Export List.

Employing two assistants in the single-room premises, Harrod's business thrived when huge crowds attended the 1851 Great Exhibition in nearby Hyde Park.

Throughout the 1850s, Charles Henry Harrod remained satisfied with his successful yet moderately sized business, but when his son, Charles Digby Harrod, took over the store in 1861, he had far grander ideas. Tea was central to his aim of expanding the business.

Charles' brother, Henry, helped in the shop between 1863 and 1866 and later wrote: "We steadily advanced especially the tea trade and built up a very nice counter trade which was, when I left it, about £200 to £250 per week and very profitable."

Soon, the business outgrew its tiny premises so, in 1879, Charles Digby Harrod bought two adjacent buildings on Brompton Road, and this led to the employment of 100 staff and the production of first-class merchandise under the new "Harrods" brand.

In December 1883, a disastrous fire broke out, and Harrods' three buildings were burned to the ground. Almost immediately after the fire, a bigger and better building rose from the ashes. Barely two years later, Harrod was employing over 200 people to service increasing customer demand.

In 1891, Richard Burbidge was appointed General Manager, and began transforming the modest store into the world-famous institution it is today. His dream was that the store occupy the entire Knightsbridge block — and by 1911 he had purchased every piece of land needed to construct the architectural masterpiece we know today. So sure was he of his vision that he approved the building of the vast facade in 1901 — *before* he had acquired all the land.

ABOVE: *Looking west along the Brompton Road to Harrods, c. 1920s.*

ABOVE: The Harrods facade today.

In the early twentieth century, tea was still an important commodity in the Harrods store and was one of its recognised specialities. When teas from the Far East arrived, they were taken to one of London's bonded warehouses where they were weighed,

... buying only the best teas ...

inspected, and auctioned. Harrods maintained its reputation by buying only the best teas at these auctions.

As the spectacular Food Halls developed and evolved, Harrods continued to give tea the prominence it deserved at the very heart of the store.

In the late 1980s, when the current Chairman, Mohamed Al Fayed implemented a storewide programme of refurbishment — which

ABOVE: The Harrods Tea Department.

has seen £400 million lavished on the building so far — an exceptional new Tea and Coffee Department was commissioned to offer Harrods customers the finest selection of teas in the world.

Each year, despite the discomforts and challenges of tropical climates, mosquitoes, difficult terrain and sometimes poor infrastructure, Harrods tea buyers travel to the best estates in their pursuit of the world's finest teas — sometimes visiting as many as a dozen remote gardens in a day.

There is often a bewildering array of fine teas, varieties and blends to choose from, but each tea is carefully and expertly sampled, before notes are compared, recommendations made, and orders placed.

ABOVE: Harrods tea buyers sampling tea varieties with the growers.

This dedication and constant striving for excellence means the Harrods customer, from the luxury of the Knightsbridge store, may confidently choose from a superb range of teas for all tastes — from a refreshing traditional English Breakfast Tea through to the world's most expensive tea: Okayti Treasure Tea, from Darjeeling.

THE TEA JOURNEY

Tea drinkers who wish to understand their favourite beverage will discover that a deeper knowledge of its origins, cultivation, and transformation into the finest quality tea is both fascinating and rewarding.

Through the efforts of growers, botanists, and sometimes even smugglers, the tea bush has spread from its original home in China to many parts of the world, such as India, Sri Lanka, Africa and South America.

Teas from these areas are like fine wines: soil, altitude and climate all combine to influence flavour and character. The finest teas, for example, grow at the highest altitude.

Achieving an optimum leaf quality requires a warm climate, constant high humidity, plenty of sunshine and regular rainfall.

The best tea is made from the "tips" or buds found at the crown of the tea bush. These tender new shoots are responsible for the distinctive aroma and quality of each tea.

Only in the hilly north Indian tea gardens of Assam and Darjeeling does the plucking season begin in March, with the arrival of refreshing light showers. The first, freshest leaves to be picked are called the

After picking, rolling, fermenting and drying, the best of these delicate buds and first leaves appear silvery or golden in colour, the sure sign of an excellent tea.

"first flush". Plucking the first flush continues until mid-April.

The period from May to mid-July brings the second flush, which

produces the most flavoursome and expensive teas. The onset of the monsoon brings a third prolific and rapid growth of new leaves, called "rain teas".

By the end of September, the monsoonal rains have passed and the season brings the fourth or "autumnal" flush during October and November.

As an example of Harrods' preference for top quality tea, even though plucking occurs throughout the year in Sri Lanka, Harrods only purchases tea plucked during the premium seasons: early February to mid-March in the east of the island; and late-June to late-August in the west. These teas are chosen from gardens in high altitude areas, such as Nuwara Eliya, Dimbula, and Uva.

Some Harrods teas, such as Ambootia Hand Rolled Tea, are only plucked during a carefully chosen two week period in June of each year.

PLUCKING

Expert plucking of tea leaves is vital to achieve tea of top quality. Only the smallest shoots, comprising two leaves and a bud, are plucked. To produce one kilogram of tea requires up to 22,000 such shoots — all plucked by hand. The very best leaves are plucked before sunrise, when the natural fragrance is at its peak, and the night's dew is still present.

Pluckers, who are almost always women, are extremely quick and skilful. Often, it is impossible to follow the motion of their hands and fingers as they pluck.

To become quality black teas, freshly plucked green tea leaves must be withered, rolled, fermented, dried and fired. Usually, the entire process takes place on the estate where the teas are grown.

WITHERING

After plucking, the green leaves are evenly spread by hand on mesh, over troughs, so that uniform withering can occur. Moisture content is lowered by about 70 percent or to a predetermined level depending on the condition of the leaf.

ROLLING

Originally, experienced estate workers rolled withered tea leaves between their palms. Two leaves and a bud were chosen and carefully hand rolled to avoid heat generation. When infused, hand-rolled leaves open up to their original state.

Harrods proudly offers an exclusive range of rare hand-rolled teas, but on most estates machinery now performs this task. Mechanical rollers gently twist the leaves and break down the cell walls, facilitating the oxidation and fermentation processes.

FERMENTING

Fermentation is a natural process that converts the raw "green" leaves into the fragrant "black" tea that tea drinkers enjoy. (Fermentation is restricted in the production of green teas, such as china tea.) This process takes place in an atmosphere of extreme humidity and stillness, where the leaves warm and ferment in the same way as barley is malted for beer. The time period and conditions of fermentation are critical to the quality of the tea. Too short a time will leave the colour pale and produce a green or semi-fermented tea; too long, and the tea will blacken and lose its flavour.

FIRING

To stop fermentation at the correct point, the tea is moved to drying bays where hot air completes the processing. This step is carefully controlled to improve storage, and also to cater to different tastes. Slightly over-fired teas, for example, tend to be quick brewing.

GRADING

A common misconception about tea is that Orange Pekoe is a particular type of tea like Darjeeling or Assam. It is, in fact, a grade of leaf, usually applied to teas from India or Sri Lanka. As the size and condition of the rolled leaf is vital to the quality and taste of the final tea, meticulous attention is paid to sorting and grading leaves into well-defined categories.

DUST

Dust refers to the very fine siftings used in most teabags.

FANNINGS

Fannings are the smallest leaves, 1-1.5 mm long, found in orthodox teas and in good quality teabags.

Due to the large surface area of the leaves, infusion should be limited to two to three minutes. In general, just over half the normal amount of tea leaves need to be added to the pot.

ORANGE PEKOE (OP)

Whole leaf teas from India or Sri Lanka, 8-15 mm long, plucked after the leaf bud has opened. They comprise this new leaf plus the top leaf from each branch.

FLOWERY ORANGE PEKOE (FOP)

Of a more delicate quality than Orange Pekoe, this tea comprises the top leaf and bud from each branch, 5-8 mm in length.

GOLDEN FLOWERY ORANGE PEKOE (GFOP)

Golden Flowery Orange Pekoe have extra tips added, which look like tiny flecks of gold. This classification applies particularly to teas from Darjeeling, where the early-plucked tender leaves retain a golden edge. These teas represent the finest quality available.

BROKEN GRADES

These leaf grades occur when whole leaves are fractured and broken in the manufacturing process. The smaller particle size leads to a stronger flavour than their whole leaf counterpart, so Broken Orange Pekoe grades, for example, have a stronger taste than Orange Pekoe.

In general, larger leaves produce a more subtle flavour, and the broken leaf grades always result in a stronger tea.

Golden tips in the leaf lead to a medium-strength tea with a flowery taste. A dash of milk may be added to Broken Orange Pekoe, Golden Broken Orange Pekoe and Fanning grades as they have a dark liquor and a more powerful taste. Orange Pekoe, Flowery Orange Pekoe, and Golden Flowery Orange Pekoe grades are usually consumed without milk.

HARRODS INDIAN TEAS

*A*t Harrods, the experts behind the counter of the Tea and Coffee Department want customers to share in the love and fascination they have for this wondrous product — sometimes described as the "eighth wonder of the world".

To excite and inspire their customers, Harrods works closely with global tea authorities to develop speciality designer teas to showcase this captivating product. In the Knightsbridge store, discerning customers can select from an unparalleled range of specialised Harrods blends, exclusive single estate teas, high quality teas from internationally recognised tea growing regions, and the purest organic teas.

The extensive range includes such luxurious items as Harrods Vintage Hand Rolled Tea, packed in limited edition hand-crafted rosewood chestlets. Hand-carved walnut chestlets made in Kashmir are also available. Harrods customers may enjoy Darjeeling Millennium Tea from Ambootia in the north of India, a distillation of over 100 years of experience and knowledge in the pursuit of perfection. They may choose Flowery Bouquet, from the Seeyok Tea Estate, a colourful mixture of fine tea blended with cornflower, marigold, rose and calendula petals.

Harrods was also amongst the first to introduce purely organic teas to the tea-drinking public. After analysing a number of premium estates, three gardens in Darjeeling and two in Assam were selected to grow Harrods organic teas in a way that minimises the impact on the environment and which allows the human communities that live and work in those gardens to thrive.

HARRODS REGIONAL TEAS

Bessagaum, a Singphoo Chief of Assam, was given some tea plants and seeds in 1823, marking the introduction of the crop to India. But the efforts of a Scottish botanist, Robert Fortune, really established India as a tea-growing region. After the Opium Wars in the first half of the nineteenth century, Fortune travelled to China, bringing prized seeds and cultivation techniques back to India.

In the following years, tea growing and processing techniques in India were refined and perfected, until the trade flourished and the best tea-growing areas of India became household names.

The best known and finest Indian regional teas are described below.

DARJEELING

Shrouded in the enigmatic mists of the majestic reaches of the Himalayas, at an elevation of 7,000 feet above sea level, is the hill resort of Darjeeling — a gift to the British from the Maharaja of Nepal. Darjeeling means "the place of Dorje", a stone or sceptre emblematic of a mystic thunderbolt. Tea plants of Chinese varieties were first planted in 1841 on the mountainous slopes around the Darjeeling area.

Darjeeling teas are known as the "champagne of teas". Darjeeling is acknowledged as the superlative

standard for flavour, unmatched anywhere else in the world. The exceptional quality of Darjeeling tea is achieved as a result of its unique combination of soil, temperature, sunshine, rainfall, mist, elevation and latitude. The region produces Regal and Maharaja class tea, each possessing a delicate muscatel taste and an enticing bouquet. Generally, Darjeeling is served without milk, but can be delicious with a slice of lemon.

DARJEELING FIRST FLUSH

When the Himalayan snows have melted, the gardens at Darjeeling begin production of the Darjeeling first flush. Harrods Darjeeling First Flush is an exclusive blend that enjoys a unique prestige in the realm of fine teas.

DARJEELING SECOND FLUSH

After the initial burst of the first flush come the flavoursome, and no less prestigious, second flush teas. All Harrods prime Darjeeling tea is bought during the second flush season which starts in May and ends by the last week of June.

ASSAM

On both sides of the mighty Brahmaputra river lie the rolling plains of Assam, where tea was first grown in India. The combination of alluvial soil and moderate rainfall makes this area ideal for tea cultivation. Today, impeccably pruned tea bushes now cover over 215,000 hectares.

The undersides of Assam leaves are characterised by an abundance of silvery, soft down, called "tip". This feature adds to the excellent quality of Assam teas.

For tea drinkers seeking a unique full-bodied strength in their tea, Harrods recommends one of their Assam blends.

HARRODS BLENDED TEAS

AFTERNOON DELIGHT TEA
When Queen Victoria was Empress of India, the wives of the tea garden owners always enjoyed a social cup of tea in the afternoon. For the ultimate in flavour, liquor, and aroma, the blend preferred by the colonial ladies was 80 percent Darjeeling and 20 percent Assam. In light of this tradition, Harrods tea experts have created Afternoon Delight tea, perfect for a relaxing afternoon tea.

EMPIRE BLEND TEA
A pioneer combination originally introduced by Harrods in 1933 for the connoisseur tea drinkers of the world, this refined blend was relaunched in 1994. Empire Blend combines Darjeeling tea with the creamy, full-bodied Assam and the flavoursome Nilgiri tea from Southern India. The result is a unique breakfast blend, representing the best from India.

BLEND 49 TEA
Blend 49 is an exotic blend encapsulating a rich heritage of Indian teas, first made to commemorate Harrods' 150th anniversary. Its unique aroma and rich flavour makes the cup perfectly desirable in every way. Moreover, the lingering taste adds to the richness of its vintage ancestry. Blend 49 is an expertly blended combination of teas from India's five main tea-producing regions. The blend is a fusion of the best characteristics from all five regions.

BREAKFAST BLEND NO. 14 TEA

More than 40 years ago, the master tea blenders at Harrods created this truly international breakfast blend by combining the finest regional teas from around the world. With high altitude Darjeeling, malty Assam, full-flavoured Ceylon, and the brightest coloured Kenyan, Breakfast Blend No. 14 is an all-round "wake-me-up" tea, and is Harrods' best selling international tea.

DARJEELING SILVER TIPS TEA

From the Himalayan heights, 6,500 feet above sea level, comes Darjeeling Silver Tips — the most flavoursome of teas. Darjeeling is the pride of Indian tea and from this mountainous region, this blend has been made from specially selected crowns, or "silver tips" — the tender parts of the shoots.

AUTUMN AROMA TEA

This tea is pure Darjeeling with only two leaves and a bud picked between the end of September and mid-October. The leaves are larger and give the tea drinker a mellow, sweet rose petal-like aroma, which is best enjoyed without milk and sugar.

ASSAM GOLDEN TIPS TEA

Assam Golden Tips comes from the plains of Brahmaputra Valley. This special Harrods tea is a blend of orthodox teas grown in the best gardens of Upper Assam. Fermentation and firing have been carefully controlled to preserve its bright golden tips. It is colourful, rich in aroma, and possesses a fresh, lingering taste.

HARRODS SINGLE ESTATE TEAS

BARI TEA

Planted by the British in the early 1800s, Okayti is an exclusive tea garden located in the Mirik Hills of the Darjeeling district. The garden grows the purest China varieties, at an optimum elevation of 4000–6200 feet above sea level.

Bari ideally combines the temperatures and mists of the Himalayas to produce an excellent quality tea. Fresh natural springs around Harrods Bari are used to irrigate the young plants.

The bushes yield special leaves that produce an exceptional quality of tea, with sparkling silver tips and an aromatic, saffron-orange cup quality.

Harrods Bari originates from a 25 hectare patch of the most special variety of pure chinery clones* from a dedicated nursery at Okayti. At an elevation of 5500 feet, Harrods

The first harvest of Harrods Bari occurred in 2002, when 2,000 kilograms of green leaves produced 500 kilograms of this most exclusive tea for Harrods.

Cloning is a method of propagation that retains the best features of both parent plants. Two China type mother bushes produce a pure China clone with the finest of flavours.

OKAYTI WONDER TEA

Available only at Harrods, Okayti Wonder Tea is a rare speciality tea created from the finest young bushes at Okayti.

Tea bushes below the age of three years are carefully selected for plucking one leaf and a bud in the early hours of the morning. Highly specialised pluckers, who take the utmost care not to damage the delicate leaves, can pluck only 200 grams of this quality of leaf

per day. A maximum of ten pluckers are deployed to bring in this exclusive leaf from the clonal sections of the estate.

The leaves are carefully transported in plucking baskets to the factory, so they are not damaged. After being carefully laid out on the withering troughs, controlled air withers the leaves for 14 hours. In wet weather, withering takes a little longer, at around 16 hours.

The leaves are lightly hand rolled by a team of five women under the most hygienic conditions. Hand rolling takes 30–40 minutes and extra care is taken to maintain the integrity of the leaves' tender tips.

After rolling, and slow fermentation, the tea is dried to eliminate any remaining moisture and seal in the magical flavour.

The whole process involves 45 workers and six managerial staff to produce just 400 grams of this exclusive tea over a two-day period.

OKAYTI SILVER PEARL TEA

Beautiful young clonal leaves with a shimmering, silvery glow are used to create Okayti Silver Pearl Tea. During the second flush, one leaf and a bud are plucked from young tender plants, pruned in the previous winter months to ensure full sap content in the new leaf.

The leaves are carefully withered for fourteen hours, after which they are gently hand rolled into delicate balls with the silver tip encircling the ball. After rolling, the leaves ferment for three hours, and are then roasted in small vessels over coal fires to ensure even drying.

This beautiful silver pearl tea has a unique flavour with a very delicate sweet taste and aroma.

OKAYTI TREASURE TEA

Okayti Treasure Tea is the finest and most exclusive tea ever produced by Okayti. One plucker, working for eight hours, can pluck only 60–80 grams of the shoots, to produce a mere 15–20 grams of finished tea.

The finest China bushes, with golden coloured leaves are carefully selected, and only the golden shoots are plucked. Of the 200,000 tea bushes growing at Okayti, only about 1,250 exhibit these extremely rare golden shoots. To catch the morning dew, high precision pluckers collect these shoots very early in the morning. If they are plucked in daylight, the shoots turn black when touched.

With great care, the shoots are transported to the factory in closed containers to prevent exposure to light.

The golden shoots are withered for ten hours, and delicately hand rolled. Fermentation, in bright sunlight, occurs for six hours. Here, the tea develops its fruity taste and bright golden look.

Since Okayti Treasure Tea was first offered in 2002, Harrods has been firm in its belief that this is the most unique and exclusive tea ever created.

AMBOOTIA WHITE TEA

Ancient secrets of tea processing, and over 140 years of experience and knowledge, combine at Ambootia to produce a unique tea, described as producing "favourable notes reminiscent of an early spring breeze".

level of antioxidants, and low tannin and caffeine levels mean that Ambootia White Tea is known as one of the healthiest teas in the world. As the least processed tea, a long brew in a lower water temperature will bring out the optimum flavour of this delightful drink.

Each spring, special species of tea bushes at Ambootia are expertly selected, and the highly skilled pluckers choose only a tender leaf with a bud for production into Ambootia White Tea.

Ambootia White Tea is an unfermented tea, retaining the original shape of its bud and leaf. The high

MARGARET'S HOPE TEA ESTATE

The estate producing Margaret's Hope Tea is a beautiful scenic garden situated close to Darjeeling. The garden is named after an English planter's daughter who died abroad before she could return to this garden — one of her favourite places.

The tea from Margaret's Hope Tea Estate is very special, producing a mellow, second flush cup with a beautiful fragrance. The tea contains a high percentage of silver tips, and the infusion is a bright golden colour. The Harrods tea comes from selected high altitude areas of this garden, where plucking is confined to dawn.

ORANGAJULI TEA ESTATE
The Orangajuli garden was established in 1894 and was so named because the *jhora* (stream) which flows alongside the factory compound is called Orang jhora. Situated near the banks of the Brahmaputra, in the state of Assam, it is one of the finest orthodox gardens in the district. During the second flush, the bushes produce extremely stylish, wiry leaves with a sprinkle of golden tips. The infusion is bright and coppery, and the liquor malty and rounded.

KHUBONG TEA ESTATE
In 2002, the Harrods team visited this Upper Assam garden and identified certain sections of the garden as producing tea with a unique and natural raspberry-like flavour. Harrods was the first to introduce this special tea to the United Kingdom.

JAMGURI TEA ESTATE
Located in the Golaghat district, this expansive plantation produces high quality CTC (Cut, Tear, Curl) and orthodox teas with an inherently bright liquor. Jamguri also produces speciality teas, such as Gold and Silver Blossom.

HAJUA TEA ESTATE

This 100 percent clonal garden, belonging to the famous Assam Company of India, produces the best clonal quality teas throughout the year. The tea has an abundance of chunky golden tips. With a golden and full-bodied liquor, the cup is smooth and has a strong, favourable aroma.

GIELLE TEA ESTATE

Situated in the Teesta Valley area, the Gielle Tea Estate is renowned as the best garden in this region, producing around 240,000 kilograms of Darjeeling tea each year. Eighty percent of this garden comprises China bush and the balance is Assam bush. The Harrods Gielle tea is plucked during the second flush from the upper hilly region, known as the Durbin area. Gielle tea has a unique flavour and all-round cup quality.

MIM TEA ESTATE

Almost a century ago, north of Darjeeling, an English couple planted this remote tea plantation. Unfortunately, the man died — but his widow managed this secluded garden very successfully for many years. It eventually became famous as the Mim garden, "Mim" being a derivation of madam or *mem sahib*.

At an altitude of 6,500 feet, in the most remote part of the sweeping Kanchunjunga Range, the garden is secluded from air pollution and continues the tradition of producing fine teas of exceptional quality.

Mim's rose-flavoured tea has an aroma that leaves one feeling refreshed. Only two leaves and a bud are carefully plucked to produce the taste of this unique Darjeeling cup of tea.

MURPHULANI TEA ESTATE

Established in 1919, the Murphulani Tea Estate was one of the earliest Assam tea gardens pioneered by Scottish planters. Flanked by the famous Nomber Wildlife Sanctuary, this picturesque estate cultivates its best 300 hectares to produce fine quality teas.

Murphulani's tea pickers pluck only two leaves and a bud, and the garden has an impeccable reputation for excellent Assam teas with brisk, full bodied flavour. Its teas are full of golden tips, which impart an unrivalled aroma.

GOOMTEE TEA ESTATE

Famous for its first flush teas, Goomtee Tea Estate consistently ranks amongst the top five Darjeeling gardens. Goomtee teas have a prominent floral bouquet and muscatel character. Adjacent

to Goomtee is Jungpana, which produces very fine second flush teas. Jungpana Upper Tea's exceptional muscatel nose is highly sought after and commands high prices.

DOOMUR DULLONG TEA ESTATE

Doomur Dullong Tea Estate is the oldest, and one the finest, tea estates in the upper Assam region. Established more than 150 years ago, this garden produces well-twisted neat leaves with chunky golden tips that result in a bright coppery infusion. The tea offers a strong aromatic cup and a taste that lingers on long after the tea has been consumed. A limited quantity of this tea is produced exclusively for Harrods.

CASTLETON TEA ESTATE

At the foothills of the Himalayas, 5,000 feet above sea level, lies Castleton, a tea garden producing highly sought after muscatel-flavoured teas. The term "muscatel" is borrowed from the sweet, strongly flavoured wine of the same name. Muscatel teas are only available for a few weeks of the year and must be plucked soon after dawn. Only teas with the choicest two leaves and a bud are selected by Harrods, to showcase the rare sweet flavour so exclusive to this estate.

SELIMBONG TEA ESTATE

With Mount Everest towering majestically in the background, sunrise at Selimbong is breathtakingly beautiful. First planted in 1866, the garden's second flush teas are eagerly anticipated by connoisseurs worldwide. Winner of the prestigious Tea Board of India's Award for Quality, Selimbong Vintage Tea is produced for only a few days in June. Having just formed into a leaf and a bud, the first shoots of the second flush are hand-picked in the early hours of the morning and processed before sunrise. This limited edition tea is produced exclusively for Harrods.

HARRODS SRI LANKAN
(CEYLON) TEAS

For an island about the size of Scotland, Sri Lanka produces 25 percent of all teas consumed on the planet.

Four degrees north of the equator, Sri Lanka's climate is ideal for tea cultivation. A combination of rich soil, pure water, vast mountainous country and fertile plains make tea production Sri Lanka's largest industry, employing one million people, and producing 277 million kilograms of tea annually.

KIRKOSWALD

On the extensive western slopes of the tea growing area in the Dimbulla region, is the most famous name in Ceylon tea, and one of the first gardens to transplant coffee with tea in the 1870s. With such a pedigree, Kirkoswald holds the record for achieving the highest prices for liquoring pekoes and Flowery Broken Orange Pekoes — as well as awards for the outstanding Ceylon Estate Tea for Dimbulla at the US Tea Association's annual tea convention.

With large, well-formed leaves, this medium-strength tea has an excellent, flowery aroma.

PETTIAGALLA

In Sabaragamuwa province, where exquisite blue sapphires are mined, lies Pettiagalla, one of Sri Lanka's most prestigious tea gardens. Pettiagalla's premium leafy grade teas, with long white tips, are favoured for their crisp, strong flavour and light cup. The unique taste leaves the mouth refreshed and cleansed.

GOWERAKELLE

Gowerakelle's green tea is grown and processed according to traditional Chinese methods. Its medicinal properties promote health, well-being and longevity. Gowerakelle's crystal clear liquor has a hue varying from orange-green to pale pink, and the monsoon season imbues it with a burst of flavour, perfect for a pleasant after dinner drink to settle the digestive system.

IDULGASHINNA

Over 5,000 feet above sea level in the Dimbulla region, Idulgashinna was originally planted with coffee during the early 1840s. After the failure of its coffee crops in the nineteenth century, tea was planted on the estate. Today, the garden produces the finest organic teas. Swathed in mist for most of the year, the upper reaches produce the finest green and black teas with a sharp, refreshing taste.

BOMBAGALLA FANNINGS

The very fine Bombagalla fannings require much less tea in the pot than other larger leaf Ceylon teas. Bombagalla fannings are ideal to produce a cup of tea that is mild but full of flavour.

HARRODS CHINA TEAS

China, the original home of tea, is now the second largest producer and third largest exporter of tea in the world. Tea has, for some 4,000 years, formed an important part of China's trade with other countries, and it continues to export an excellent variety of black teas, green teas, semi-fermented teas, smoked teas and perfumed teas.

Unlike India and Ceylon, the system in China is based on large co-operatives, where domestic blending of teas from each distinctive region ensures continuity and consistency of taste and aroma. For this reason, none of Harrods China teas carries the name of the individual garden.

BLACK CHINA TEA (UNSMOKED)

RUSSIAN CARAVAN

As early as 1618, the Russian Czar enjoyed tea presented to him by the Chinese Embassy. In 1689, free trade between Russia and China began, in the form of large

groups, or caravans, of camels laden with exotic goods. One of the most prized commodities was tea, blended by the caravan masters from teas purchased along their route.

As each caravan master had his own secret recipe and sources of supply, every caravan tea has its own distinctive qualities and flavour. Harrods Russian Caravan is a blend of medium-strength China teas that produces relaxing and warming flavours with a touch of smokiness.

KEEMUN

Keemun is a light tea, ideally drunk black, with or without lemon. It is often used as the base for fruit-flavoured teas.

KEEMUN CONGOU

This is the finest quality Keemun tea. It is naturally low in caffeine and therefore ideal as a late evening drink.

YUNNAN

Much prized for its health-giving characteristics, Yunnan tea is the only China tea with enough body to take the addition of milk.

CHING WOO

A unique black tea for connoisseurs who enjoy its slight chocolate after-taste.

BLACK CHINA TEA (SMOKED)

LAPSANG SOUCHONG

At Harrods, this popular smoked China tea is available as China White Point. This favoured tea represents the very best of Lapsang Souchong, as it contains the delicate white points of the tea bush. The black smoked tea variety known as Tarry Souchong is the smokiest of all the teas.

CHINA GUNPOWDER

"Gunpowder" refers to this tea's appearance, as the tea leaves are rolled into small ball-shaped pellets resembling old-fashioned gunpowder. These pellets expand enormously when infused.

China Gunpowder Tea has a very delicate aroma and taste, and imparts a pale greenish-gold liquor.

HARRODS INFUSIONS

arrods fruit-flavoured teas are a blend of fine Chinese, Indian and Ceylon teas, flavoured with the highest quality natural fruit oils. As the flavour may dissipate after a few months, these teas are best bought in small quantities.

Usually drunk without milk, fruit-flavoured teas are equally delicious served as iced teas. A range of the popular Harrods varieties are described in this chapter.

POUCHKINE TEA

Pouchkine is a blend of Sri Lankan, Assam and China teas, flavoured predominantly with oil of berg-amot. Differentiated from Earl Grey by the addition of natural cit-rus oils such as grapefruit, orange and lemon, this tea is delicious when served as iced tea.

FOUR SEASONS TEA

Four Seasons is a blend of China teas with the subtle addition of peaches, pears, citrus fruits and hazelnuts.

VICTORIAN ROSE TEA

Victorian Rose is a China black tea flavoured with Bulgarian rose oils of the finest quality.

MYSTERY TEA

Mystery Tea is a mixture of black teas from China and Sri Lanka which is flavoured with vanilla and lavender extracts, crushed vanilla pods, and orange, tangerine, and lemon oils to create the aura of mystery around this tea.

CHRISTMAS TEA

Christmas Tea, the perfect seasonal drink, is a mixture of Ceylon and China teas blended with hibiscus, orange peel, caramel, Marasquino, pineapple and spices, giving it a traditional yuletide flavour.

GREEN MINT TEA

Harrods Green Mint Tea is an unfermented leaf tea, rolled into balls and flavoured with Moroccan *nanah* mint (considered to be the highest quality mint available). This authentic green mint tea should be drunk very hot and sweet, as a dessert.

JASMINE TEA

Adding just the right amount of jasmine flowers to a high-quality China tea produces a delicate and flowery flavour. Harrods Jasmine Tea is ideally served black, and is a perfect companion to traditional Chinese food.

FOUR FRUITS TEA

Four Fruits is a popular and refreshing blend of Sri Lankan, Indian and China teas subtly flavoured with cherry, strawberry, raspberry and redcurrant.

HERBAL TEAS

Harrods Herbal Teas do not contain any tea. Instead, they consist entirely of the leaves or flowers of the plant indicated. Herbal teas are known for their health-giving properties and, under expert guidance, may be used to assist many minor ailments.

Harrods offers a full range of herbal teas. Some of the more popular teas include Spearmint, Camomile, Lemon Verbena, Peppermint and Rosehip.

FRUIT INFUSIONS

Harrods Fruit Infusions are produced from the best quality dried fruits and flowers, blended together to make a delicious caffeine-free infusion.

Among the broad selection available are Rosehip, Camomile and Mixed Fruity.

Fruit infusions provide a healthy alternative to traditional tea and coffee when preferring to avoid caffeine and tannin. Loose fruit infusions are convenient, completely natural, and generally give a deeper colour and more intense flavour than teabags.

THE PERFECT CUP OF TEA

Anna, the Duchess of Bedford (1788–1861), is credited with introducing the concept of "afternoon tea" to Britain. Regularly inviting her friends to enjoy a light meal, tea, and conversation at around five p.m., the Duchess's idea quickly spread through London society.

Today, of course, a perfect cup of tea is welcome at any time of day — and it doesn't need to be silver service to be enjoyed!

The first step in preparing a perfect cup of tea is to ensure that the tea is stored in a cool, dry place separate from other goods

that may contaminate its aroma or flavour. Harrods speciality teas are supplied in attractive, airtight, light-proof caddies to ensure the leaves remain fresh. If the tea is exposed to the air some of the flavour and aroma will be lost, eventually impairing the taste. Ideally the container should be metallic or ceramic, not plastic or glass. Tea should never be refrigerated.

The next step is to transform the leaves into a golden, refreshing cup of tea. There is one thing the British agree upon and that is the time-honoured method of producing a flavoursome cup of tea.

To achieve the best results from tea, whether using teabags or leaf tea, it is important to use freshly drawn water. Warm the teapot by rinsing it with boiling water. When using leaf tea, use one heaped teaspoon of tea per cup, and one for the pot. Pour freshly boiled water into the pot, and allow it to brew for 2–3 minutes for Darjeeling, and 3–5 minutes for other teas and blends. Gently stir, and decant using a strainer.

When brewing green tea, water should be boiled then cooled to around 80–85 degrees Celsius. Tea should be added at the rate of one teaspoon of tea per cup of water, and one teaspoon for the pot. While most green teas brew for 2–3 minutes some, such as Shincha, require only 45–60 seconds.

For iced tea, pour hot water over double the amount of tea used for hot tea. After brewing for about three minutes, add enough ice to double the volume. After a further three minutes, pour the liquid over more ice, and serve.

With black teas, a slice of lemon, or orange, or milk may be added. Sweeten with sugar or honey, as desired.

Or, indeed, you may simply wish to pay heed to the mischievous advice of a nineteenth century British observer who wrote:

"Love and scandal are the best sweeteners of tea."

ENJOY!

A GUIDE TO TRADEMARKS

Today, just as with fine wines which operate under a system of Denomination Control, the Tea Board of India uses a number of trademarks of origin to signal a guarantee of quality and origin to the consumer. Harrods was amongst the first to use these trademarks when they were first introduced.

These trademarks are only awarded to teas of guaranteed origin which meet stringent standards of flavour, body and bouquet specified by the Tea Board of India's tasters.

Many of the Indian trademarks, such as Darjeeling, denote tea that is picked and packed in the region, guaranteeing the freshness of the leaves for the consumer.

In its efforts to ensure that connoisseurs of premier Indian teas get value for money and enjoy the true taste of Indian teas year after year, the India Tea trademark appears only on teas that are packed in India. The Tea Board of India guarantees the freshness of the leaves and therefore the quality of the tea.

Darjeeling
Region Logo

Tea Board of
India Logo

Assam is known as the land of the one-horned rhinoceros, and the rhinoceros trademark can only be used when the package contains 100 percent Assam teas.

At Harrods, fine Sri Lankan and Bangladeshi teas are guaranteed by a strictly controlled system of originating trademarks.

Harrods organic teas also carry their own trademark.

Assam Region Logo

Sri Lankan Tea
Logo

BANGLADESH TEA

Bangladeshi Tea
Logo

Harrods
Organic Logo

Certificate of Excellence

Tea Board of India
awards
this Certificate of Excellence
to
Harrods of Knightsbridge,
London
on their 150th Anniversary
in recognition of their presenting to discerning
Customers
the Finest Selection of
High Quality Indian Teas.

Chairman
Tea Board of India

13th August, 1999

LEFT: On the occasion of its 150th anniversary, Harrods' unique association with the tea trade was recognised with a special Certificate of Excellence from the Tea Board of India.